HELMING
TO WIN

HELMING TO WIN

Lawrie Smith
and Ian Pinnell

fernhurst **BOOKS**

Copyright © Fernhurst Books 1994

First published in 1994 by Fernhurst Books, Duke's Path,
High Street, Arundel, West Sussex, BN18 9AJ, UK

Printed and bound in Great Britain

British Library Cataloguing in Publication Data:
A catalogue record for this book is available from the British Library.

ISBN 1-898660-01-8

Acknowledgements

The publishers would like to thank Andy Hemmings for crewing Ian
Pinnell in most of the photos. Paul Brotherton of Hyde Sails kindly loaned
the 470, and Adrian Jones of the Laser Centre kindly provided the Laser
5000. All other boats were owned and prepared by Ian Pinnell.

Hayling Island Sailing Club generously allowed us to use their facilities for
the shoot, and Frank Dunster kindly drove his rescue boat as a camera
craft.

Photographic credits
All photographs by John Woodward & Tim Hore except:
Crystel Clear: page 2
Roger Lean-Vercoe: pages 8, 29, 78, 80, 88
Pickthall Picture Library: page 55
Kos: page 72

DTP by TT Designs
Cover design by Simon Balley
Printed and bound by Ebenezer Baylis & Son, Worcester
Text set in 10pt Rockwell Light

CONTENTS

INTRODUCTION

Before the start of any campaign you must decide how successful you want to be and to what lengths you are prepared to go to achieve this success. If you are already a good club helmsman sailing every weekend, you may only need to improve your techniques slightly to be in the top 15 at your National Championships. If, however, you want to be National Champion, you must put a great deal more time and effort into gaining your objective. So, decide first what your aim is and whether it is possible to commit enough time and finance to achieve it.

One of the most difficult tasks is assessing your own potential, because if you do not have some natural talent it will be very hard to win a National title in one of

the big popular classes. Having said that, don't despair – anyone who spends sufficient time and money will not be very far from the number one spot if he or she goes about the job in the right way.

Assuming you have decided to win the National title in your class, you must have the following resources:

1 A first – class crew who is the correct weight and size for the boat, is fit and agile, has sufficient racing experience and the time and money to support himself for the duration of the campaign.

2 A boat and equipment at least as good as any rival's.

3 Tuning data (either your own, or supplied by your sailmaker) compatible with your rig. You will be perfecting these measurements as you train.

4 Time and finance to support an all-year campaign, sailing most weekends winter and summer, plus one night a week and three weeks of championships.

5 One or two nights a week on boat maintenance and preparation.

6 Enough races under your belt to give you a good feel for strategy, tactics and the rules.

If you can achieve all these, the rest is determination, effort and the skills outlined in this book.

Part One of this book explains the techniques you must master during your practice sessions. The objective is to show you how to make the boat go as fast as possible in all conditions of wind and sea. For most of the manoeuvres we describe first how to handle the boat in medium winds and then show how to modify this for light and heavy airs.

Part Two looks at the race itself and how you can apply your helming skills to win.

Part Three is a masterclass. In it you will learn what is important in a campaign: time management, attitude, boat preparation, boatspeed and feel. And a troubleshooting chapter highlights what to do when your speed is poor.

How large an improvement should you be looking for? The difference in distance between twentieth place and first place in most major championships is very small, usually 200 to 300 yards. Therefore you need only improve your performance by a fraction of one per cent to gain twenty places. Don't look for overnight success by simply buying new sails or boats, but work at the finer points and, eventually, you will edge your way towards the front. There is no magic formula, only a lot of painstaking work with boat and crew, gradually eliminating errors, improving techniques and bringing the boat to its best for the big week. It will also help to find a tuning partner so you can together practice manoeuvres such as tacking and gybing, and can do boat tuning runs and log the fastest settings.

The authors. Left: Lawrie Smith. Above: Ian Pinnell (crewed by Andy Hemmings) enjoying the photo session.

HELMING TECHNIQUES

1 BEATING IN FLAT WATER

BEATING IN MEDIUM WINDS

Conditions Flat open water, 6 to 15 knots of wind, and the best boat and rig available.

Objectives To make the best VMG (velocity made good) to the weather mark. You are out to find the best compromise between speed through the water and pointing ability.

The rig In these conditions the boat must be pointing as close to the wind as possible.

A tension device is a vital aid to tuning. Since they vary you must have your own; indeed two is better, so one can be kept as a master and the other used until it wears out.

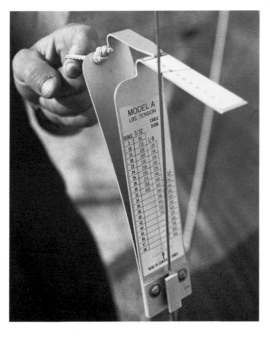

There are no waves to stop you and speed is easily achieved and maintained; therefore sails must be set reasonably flat with a small amount of twist. The mainsail is sheeted with the aft end of the boom as close to the centreline as possible and the jib is set on its innermost fairlead position. Standing rigging must be tight: 330 to 400 pounds on the jib luff wire is ideal for most classes, but check your class tuning sheet first. Note that for lower stretch shrouds (rod or Dyform) you have to use the gauge on the jib luff, but on 1 x 19 conventional stays it's common to measure the shroud tension.

Boat trim The boat at all times must be kept absolutely level: anything other than a slight heel to windward will slow you down. If the boat does heel, everything starts working against you.

1 The centreboard will be less efficient if it is not vertical.

2 The air will be diverted and disturbed by flowing over the topsides of the hull before it reaches the lower sections of the sails.

3 In almost all dinghy classes the hull is designed to be more efficient when level. This gives maximum waterline length, and is particularly important in non-planing conditions.

4 The heel of the boat will create too much weather helm, making the rudder act as a brake.

Beating in medium winds. The boat is well balanced and the boom is on the centreline.

bow is too far out of the water it will tend to get blown away from the wind and pointing will suffer.

Rake Correct rake is vital, particularly on high performance boats where a large range of rake is needed. Check your tuning sheet - you should be near the middle of the range, gradually raking aft more to keep the boat in balance as the wind builds.

Centreboard In these conditions it pays to angle the board up to 15 degrees forwards in 6 knots, gradually moving it upright as the wind builds to 15 knots. This helps the boat point closer to the wind by moving the centre of effort forwards. The reason for moving the board is so that the mast doesn't

Before attempting to sail the boat upright you first have to learn the technique. Most sailors believe their boats are level when in fact they are still heeled 5 or 10 degrees. The best way to perfect the technique is to fit a clinometer to the front bulkhead and get the feel of sailing upright. This will give you a good indication of your sideways trim, as will studying the flow of water off the stern of the boat. You will see a disturbance off the leeward quarter if you are heeled.

   For correct fore and aft trim, the helm and crew must be as close together as possible, the crew's back foot or (if not trapezing) body touching the helmsman, leaving only enough room for the movement of his mainsheet arm. The crew's forward foot should be positioned 9 to 12 inches behind the shroud, the idea being to keep maximum waterline length and to stop the stern digging. Also if the

The effect of heel is to increase weather helm (note the tiller angle) and drag from the leeward quarter (shown by the quarter wave).

Handling the mainsheet and tiller. Left: in light airs it works well to have the tiller beside you. Right: once you're hiking have the tiller across your body so you can adjust the mainsheet quickly.

The mainsheet controls the leech: (left) correct, (centre) too loose giving an open leech, (right) too tight giving a closed leech.

have to be raked excessively to induce enough weather helm when the boat is upright. Of course, if the boat is allowed to heel then you will have too much helm.

Mainsheet and vang The sail must be kept reasonably flat with little twist. Try to achieve this with the mainsheet, pulling until the top telltale is stalling 30% of the time. Vang tension is to be avoided because it

reduces power in the mainsail by over-bending the lower half of the mast and opening the top of the mainsail. Just take up the slack so the sail stays in control when the mainsheet is slackened for gusts or for tacking.

Outhaul For flat water ease the outhaul only half an inch from the black band, to stop the lower leech hooking to windward.

The outhaul controls the lower leech: (above left) a tight outhaul opens the lower leech, (above right) a slack outhaul closes the lower leech.

A tight cunningham (below left) pulls the draft forward, opens the lower leech and twists off the top of the leech. A loose cunningham (below right) has the opposite effect.

Tiller and rudder The tiller extension must be long enough for you to be able to steer while sitting up against the shroud in light winds. Any longer or shorter is no good. When sitting on the deck (as against hiking out) it is better to hold the tiller by your side, otherwise the tip of the extension will become tied up in the mainsheet. When hiking hold it in front of you so that you can use your tiller hand on the mainsheet when adjusting the vang, cunningham, etc.

Rudder movements should never be

Correct jib setting: adjust sheet tension and fairlead position to give an ideal slot.

excessive as you are not forcing the boat down a wave or trying to promote planing. Accurate and sensitive movements are the best, steering the straightest and shortest course according to changes in the wind.

Cunningham As a rule, never use the cunningham unless overpowered. From 6 - 8 knots leave it slack, or you will pull the flow forward and choke the slot. Don't worry about the horizontal creases running out of the luff behind the mast. From 10 knots up, pulling the cunningham opens the upper mainsail leech and holds the flow forward.

Steering Pointing and speed are related. If you are going slowly but pointing high you may appear to be going in a good direction but you will also be making more leeway than someone who is not pointing as high but going faster. It is, therefore, very important to achieve maximum speed before trying to point. You should have telltales on the luff of the jib at one-third, half, and two-thirds luff length. Get all these streaming, with the weather ones just beginning to 'break', then steer as accurately as possible to them. Your mainsail should have telltales positioned on or around each batten pocket. For most classes, sheet the main until the top telltale is beginning to break. But in classes such as the 505 the top telltale streams all the time and the next one down is kept on the break.

Gusts and lulls In medium winds your crew should always be trapezing, even if this means you have to sit on the deck rather than hike. The benefits are:

1   Extra support for the mast (more power).

2   Better vision for helmsman and crew.

3 Trapezing enables the helmsman and crew to get closer together, with the crew's back foot behind the helmsman.

4 The crew can stretch or bend very quickly to the changes in the wind speed. As soon as the wind will support him your crew should be out on the trapeze wire. Ensure the trapeze handles are high (when the crew is trapezing at his lowest level he should just be able to reach the handle). Trapezing high will help him get out sooner. As a gust hits, the crew is the first to move, extending himself outwards to counteract the extra pressure. If this is not sufficient he should lower himself using the trapeze adjuster. Finally he can put his arms behind his head to produce more leverage. Meanwhile the helmsman should ease his bodyweight over the side while at the same time hardening closer to the wind

For correct fore-and-aft trim the helmsman and crew should concentrate their weight at mid length and keep very close together, with the crew's foot 9-12 inches behind the shroud.

and releasing the mainsheet. If necessary, pull on some vang to control the leech.

In a lull, the first to move is the helmsman who should come in from the hiked position. If you are not hiking, then the crew should raise himself higher on the trapeze and then bend his knees, not his back. At the same time, both sheets should be eased and possibly the vang too so the telltale on the leech of the main is kept on the break.

Concentration Concentration at all times must be 100 per cent. Anything short of this will result in your losing speed or missing a shift. The more you practice the easier it becomes; you are trying to make fast sailing second nature. Try not to get too tense or nervous as this will make you stiff and clumsy around the boat, gripping the tiller too hard or pulling the mainsheet in too tight. Attention must be paid to setting your sails correctly - once again with practice this becomes much easier. Watching telltales and trim is important, but there is no substitute for time on the water to give a complete feel for the boat, and you should be able to steer to within 2 or 3 degrees of the wind with your eyes closed.

To get a good slot on a wide boat, sheet the jib close and ease the main.

When you can do this you can then concentrate more on shifts, the compass and your competitors.

You and your crew should always have a note of the compass readings on both tacks. If you do get a header then wait for four or five seconds before tacking to make sure it is a genuine shift.

Going slowly Common mistakes are:

1 Oversheeting of sails (stalling the leeches).

2 Making the sails too full, especially by pushing the lower mast back with a strut or chocks which straightens the lower mast and chokes the slot.

3 Thinking you are going slowly when in fact boats around are in a different wind or are, in reality, no faster than you.

Non-trapeze boats In most classes of two-man dinghy the above principles apply. In the Enterprise class the rule prevents you from sheeting the jib close enough to the centreline, forcing you to have a very flat sail which must then be sheeted much harder and never eased more than one inch. Mainsails are also much fuller because of the wider slot, and need to be sheeted further outboard 4 to 5 inches off the centreline.

Keep the boat upright at all times and make sure your crew is never in your line of vision. If the wind isn't strong enough for him to hike, then get him to lie (rather than sit) on the deck, improving your vision and reducing windage. As the wind builds, keep the boat flat by easing the mainsheet and feathering the boat into the wind. Now use vang tension to control the leech and keep the top telltale on the break.

BEATING IN LIGHT WINDS

Conditions Flat open water, and 0 to 6 knots of wind.

The rig The vital thing in light winds is to keep the air flowing around the sails. If they are too full the wind won't have enough energy to bend around the excessive camber. Therefore both mainsail and jib must be set as flat as possible, with a little more twist than in medium winds. This can be achieved by pre-bending the mast near deck level with a mast puller. On those classes that prohibit pullers, or have deck-stepped masts, angle the spreaders aft to produce pre-bend. Tie the top batten with very little tension to keep the head of the sail flat. Use 330 to 400 lb of rig tension and move the jib fairleads aft to flatten the sail and open up the leech.

Boat trim As the wind builds, keep the boat flat by easing the mainsheet and feathering the boat into the wind. Now use vang tension to control the leech and keep the top telltale on the break. In winds under 2 knots a slight heel to leeward will pay by reducing wetted surface area, increasing weather helm and 'feel', and helping to keep the sails set. The helm and the crew should be positioned as far forward as possible with the crew against the shroud, so keeping the stern out of the water. Never let your crew sit to leeward of the centreboard case; instead you must sit further in, so keeping your weights closer together. In 3 to 6 knots get your crew to trapeze as early as possible; this will mean your sitting on the inside of the side tank and the crew trapezing very high.

Rake Put the mast in its most upright position. It is now stiffer, because the spreaders are supporting it, so use prebend controls and angle the spreaders back (if possible) to keep the mainsail flat.

Centreboard Angle the centreboard forwards up to 15 degrees as in medium winds to create weather helm.

Mainsheet and vang In 0 to 2 knots use no vang and no mainsheet tension. The boom will be slightly off-centre but at least the leech won't hook above the centreline and stall. In 3 to 6 knots set the boom on the centreline using no vang and as little mainsheet as possible.

In 5 knots the crew must be out of the slot, and you should both have your weight forward. Bottom: if the wind drops lighter, the crew will need to move to leeward to help the sails fill, while still keeping as low as possible.

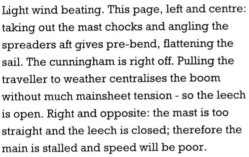
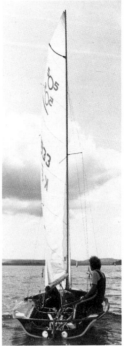

Light wind beating. This page, left and centre: taking out the mast chocks and angling the spreaders aft gives pre-bend, flattening the sail. The cunningham is right off. Pulling the traveller to weather centralises the boom without much mainsheet tension - so the leech is open. Right and opposite: the mast is too straight and the leech is closed; therefore the main is stalled and speed will be poor.

Outhaul Pull the clew out to the black band to flatten the lower third of the mainsail as much as possible.

Tiller and rudder If the wind is under 4 knots (non-trapezing) hold your tiller extension lightly by your side and adjust to wind changes with smooth movements.

Cunningham Fully released.

Steering If the telltales aren't working concentrate on the first 6 inches of the jib luff. Luff occasionally to ensure you're on the wind, with the luff of the jib lifting 10% of the time. If you slow down speed will take a long time to build back up, so don't pinch.

Gusts and lulls As a gust hits, you and your crew should move outboard as in medium winds, tighten the jibsheet to compensate and pull the mainsail in with the mainsheet. Generally don't cleat the mainsheet, as in these airs you can feel the wind through the sail's `pull'. Set the mainsail so that the top streamer is just beginning to break. If the wind drops very light ease the sheets to create more twist, and heel the boat to leeward.

Concentration Concentrate on keeping your movements around the boat down to a minimum. Any disturbance will shake the rig and slow you down. Pay more attention to the strength of wind rather than its direction. Get your crew to be on a constant look-out for more wind and always sail in the direction from where the new

the boom as close to the centreline as possible (which opens the slot).

Because these boats travel fast, they need flat, twisted sails. This is achieved by raking the mast aft: the spreader geometry changes so the mast bends, flattening the sail and opening the leech. However, don't let off too much strut (or remove too many chocks) or the bottom mast will bend, reducing lower leech return and killing pointing ability. In fact leaving the strut/chocks in the medium setting will often do, because the mast moves back with increased rake. Since techniques vary from class to class, use two-boat tuning to check the fastest settings.

Boat trim Sail the boat absolutely upright with the crew trapezing low enough to be just skimming the water. You should be hiked out as far as possible but in a comfortable enough position to play the mainsheet and steer the boat efficiently. Keep your weights together, with the crew's front foot 18 to 24 inches behind the shroud.

Rake Maximum rake, which should be increased even more for light crews. This will help you to keep the boat upright and stop her luffing in the gusts.

Centreboard Gradually raise the centreboard to keep the boat balanced. With maximum mast rake the centreboard will be angled aft 15 degrees.

Mainsheet and vang Use vang tension to control the twist in the sail. As the top streamer will be flowing all the time pull the vang progressively harder until you are no longer overpowered. If the mast isn't stiff enough, horizontal creases will appear out of the luff behind the mast before you have sufficient leech tension. Use more chocks or rake the spreaders further forward.

wind or more wind is likely to come, even if this means sailing through windshifts.

Going slowly The most common cause of bad speed in light airs is incorrect sail shape. Remember, keep the sails as flat as possible, ease the sheets, try to relax and keep still in the boat.

Non-trapeze boats All the same principles apply. When the wind increases you should concentrate on boatspeed, leaving your crew to balance the boat.

BEATING IN HEAVY WINDS

Conditions Flat open water, and 16 to 35 knots of wind.

The rig For high performance boats in these winds the rig must be adjusted to prevent the boat being overpowered, to keep her in balance, and to help you keep

Beating in heavy airs. Left: use maximum rake. Centre: try to keep the boom on the centreline as much as possible to keep the slot open. Right: that spray's cold!

Outhaul Tight!

Tiller and rudder The rudder must be vertical; if not, the helm will become heavy and weather helm increase. Hold the tiller in front of you and be very positive about the direction you want the boat to go.

Cunningham Pull on enough tension to remove the creases forming behind the mast. If you are still overpowered pull on more as this will move the draft forward and open the top third of the mainsail.

Steering In these winds, speed is more important than pointing high. Always keep the boat going fast; if you do slow down pressure on the sails increases and you

become overpowered and end up throwing away valuable energy by easing sheets.

Gusts and lulls As a gust hits, ease the mainsheet while keeping the boat going straight. When the boat has reached its new speed pull the main back in and head up closer to the wind. A `swooping' course should be steered through the gusts and lulls. In a big squall ease both sheets to keep the slot open and the boat balanced.

Concentration Concentrate on keeping the boat level and going fast, adjusting the sails constantly to the changes in wind speed. Make sure you get into the right shift sequence as extra tacks will cost you three or four boat lengths.

Going slowly Make sure you have the correct rig tension as a sagging jib luff closes the slot and makes the entry of the sail too full. Adjust the mainsheet constantly

in gusty conditions, as a heel to leeward will reduce speed dramatically.

Non-trapeze boats Because there is not the same leverage without a trapeze, `powering' the boat along will not pay unless you have a heavy all-up crew weight. Therefore in a gust keep the jib sheeted in tight and steer to keep the windward telltale breaking continuously. Meanwhile ease the mainsheet to keep the boat flat. You will find you are playing the mainsheet constantly (for fast response don't use ratchet blocks). Don't raise the centreboard unless the conditions are severe as it will prevent you from pointing (with the jib sheeted in tight the bow will tend to be blown away from the wind).

Mistakes in heavy airs (below). The mast is too upright and the boom too far out.

2 BEATING THROUGH WAVES

BEATING THROUGH WAVES IN MEDIUM WINDS

Conditions Five-foot high waves, 50 feet between crests and 6 to 15 knots of wind.

The rig In these conditions maximum power is required from the rig. Fuller sails are required to power the boat through the chop, and a fuller entry prevents the sails stalling. This is achieved by slightly more pusher (more chocks) and less vang and mainsheet tension. The top telltale should be streaming most of the time. Move the jib fairleads further forward than the setting for flat water. Keep the rig tension at 330 to 400lb.

Boat trim Helmsman and crew should be as close together as possible with the crew's forward foot 6 inches further aft than in flat water. Sail the boat level. Both the helmsman and crew should move far enough aft going down the waves to stop the bow burying in a trough, and then forward as they begin rising up the next wave to help the boat over the new crest and on down the next wave. Because there is less wind in the troughs than on the crests, your crew will have to move inboard by bending his knees to compensate for the reduction in power. In extreme sea conditions you will also have to come in from a hiked position to one of sitting on the deck. Once the boat begins to climb up the new wave both of you should move back outboard and at the same time forward, to keep the boat level.

Mainsheet and vang Set the vang so that the mainsheet is controlling the leech tension but the vang takes the load the moment you ease the mainsheet. Keep the boom on the centreline at the stern. Play the sheet constantly, easing it out as you go down a wave and pulling it back in as you climb the next one.

Outhaul Ease the outhaul by 1 inch.

Steering A `swooping' course through the waves must be steered to produce maximum speed in these conditions. To achieve this you must steer closer to the wind as the boat climbs the wave (windward telltale just lifting) and, on reaching the top, bear away for the descent. As you begin the climb to the top, boat speed decreases and pressure on the sails increases as you approach the crest. You must, therefore, steer closer to the wind to counteract this extra force while, at the same time, hiking and trapezing as effectively as possible. As you reach the top, bear away, ease enough mainsheet to keep the boat level and accelerate down the wave into the next trough. As you reach the bottom, pull the sheet back in and head up into the next wave once more.

Concentration Concentrate at all times on keeping the boat moving fast, because if you take a wave badly you will lose several boat lengths. It is better to steer around a bad wave and give away distance to windward rather than stop the boat by slamming into it. As you weave around the waves keep a constant check on your compass as this is your only way in these conditions of detecting a shift.

BEATING THROUGH WAVES IN HEAVY WINDS

Conditions Six to eight foot waves, 80 to 100 feet between crests, and 15 to 28 knots of wind.

The rig This should be set up as for flat water except it pays to open the slot by moving the jib fairlead outboard (or back).

Boat trim Both helm and crew should move further aft with the crew's back foot level with the mainsheet block. Again both should move forward and back, going up and down the waves, with the boat kept absolutely level.

This Laser Worlds was sailed in a huge swell.

Centreboard Lift the centreboard by 20 degrees to reduce weather helm in the gusts.

Steering Steer the same course as in medium winds with both sheets eased out more. If you are still overpowered move the jib fairleads progressively back or outboard until you are in control. Keep the boat moving at maximum speed and don't try to steer too close to the wind as this will only push you sideways (to leeward).

BEATING THROUGH WAVES IN LIGHT WINDS

Conditions Three to six foot waves, 25 to 30 feet between crests, and 0 to 6 knots of wind.

The rig Settings should be the same as in flat water except move the jib fairleads 1 inch further forward and ease the sheet 1 inch to give a slightly fuller and more powerful sail.

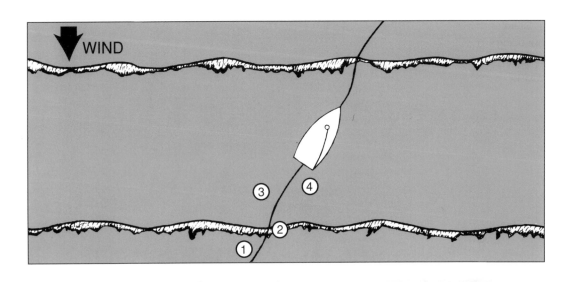

2. On the crest of the wave bear away, and both move your weight forward.

1. As the boat goes up the wave, move your weight back and begin to luff, while the crew also steps back.

4. Head up again in the trough and sheet in ready for the next wave.

3. Ease the mainsheet to accelerate down the back of the wave, with your crew trapezing flat out. For a large wave, ease the jib as well as the main.

Boat trim Helmsman and crew should position themselves as close together as possible with the crew's forward foot 6 inches behind the shroud going up the waves, and moving aft going down into the troughs. Don't ease the mainsheet when going down the waves as you will be throwing energy away. Instead both you and your crew should be alert and ready to hike or trapeze to keep the boat level as she accelerates down each wave.

Mainsheet and vang These controls should be set in the same way as for flat water.

Steering Steer the same 'swooping' course as in medium winds, keeping the boat moving at all times.

BEATING THROUGH A CHOP

Conditions Three foot waves, 15 feet between crests.

The rig Set up the boat to produce maximum power from the rig as described earlier. Move the jib fairlead 2 inches further forward than in flat water and ease the sheet 1 inch to produce a more powerful shape. Keep the rig tension on 300 to 350 lb.

Boat trim These are certainly the most difficult conditions to sail in and a great deal of practice is required to perfect your technique. Helmsman and crew should

Hold the boat upright at all times and keep the power on to ensure that she drives through the confused water. Keep your bodies close together to let the bow and stern ride easily over the waves. Steer constantly to present the bow head on to each wave.

position themselves as close together as possible with the crew's back foot level with the traveller. If a really big wave is approaching the crew must step further aft, stepping forward again if the waves ahead become smaller. Sail the boat level, and in smaller seas a heel to windward will pay.

Centreboard The centreboard should be all the way down unless you are overpowered, in which case raise it 2 inches.

Mainsheet, traveller and vang Set the mainsail with the mainsheet controlling leech tension and cleat the vang so that it comes into effect for the tacks only. Play the traveller in the gusts, pulling it up as you head into each wave and easing it back down as you bear away. If you do 'take' a wave badly and slow down, ease the mainsheet to create more twist in the sail and only pull it back in when the boat is up to full speed.

Steering The technique for sailing through a chop is very similar to sailing in a swell; the major difference is the speed at which your rudder operates. As you hit each crest your boat's bow must be turning into the wave, striking it as square as possible. This is because the waves will be coming down towards you in the same direction as the wind and will, consequently, be slamming onto your weather bow. By presenting your boats 'sharp point' to the wave you reduce resistance. As soon as you have headed into the wave and got your bow through it bear away to gather speed ready for the next one. Steering a zig-zag course like this will, if done properly, result in a faster course over the ground than simply steering straight and letting each wave slam into the side of the boat with a sickening thud.

3 TACKING

A tack in itself if a fairly simple operation, but to perfect it requires many hours of practice alone. In anything other than the lightest of winds tacking will always lose you distance and it is, therefore, vital that your tacks are perfect. Try to arrange the boat so that your crew tacks facing forwards. This is quicker, because he can see the new jibsheet and trapeze handle.

However helmsmen must note that it is always better to tack slowly rather than quickly.

TACKING IN MEDIUM WINDS

Conditions Six to 15 knots of wind.

The approach Assume you are beating hard on the wind, fully hiked and your crew flat out on the trapeze. First warn your crew

that you are considering a tack. He can then generally prepare himself and unhook, so making the manoeuvre quicker. When you eventually decide to tack shout "Let's go" or words to that effect. Steer the boat into the wind, leaving the mainsheet cleated or holding it with the same amount of tension. As your crew comes in off his trapeze he should sheet the jib in harder, sit down on the deck and begin to step over the centreboard case towards the other side. You should by then be pushing the boat further into the wind. As you reach `head to wind' both of you should cross the boat as quickly and smoothly as possible. Your crew should back the jib enough to help the boat around so that you can avoid excessive rudder movement. The backed jib also helps roll the boat to weather. Once on the new tack your crew should pull the jib in gradually but not completely with one

hand while swinging out onto the trapeze handle with his other hand. When he is out over the side he should hook on and pull the jib in to its marked position. At the same time you will have crossed the boat, eased enough mainsheet to keep the boat in balance and be fully hiked before pulling the mainsheet back in, in unison with the jib.

Changing hands on tiller and mainsheet Assume you are on starboard tack, your tiller in your left hand and the mainsheet in your right. Push the tiller across the boat and keep hold of sheet and tiller with the same hands. Cross the boat while turning, facing forwards, still with sheet and tiller in the same hands. When you reach the other side, sit down; your tiller will still be in your left hand behind your back, and your mainsheet in your right. Slide your right hand along the sheet until you are holding both sheet and tiller in that hand. Then take your left hand from behind your back and grasp the sheet.

Coming out of the tack If the boat is roll tacked smoothly, very little speed is lost and your wakes should be at 90 degrees.

But if you have tacked too quickly you will steer an 'S' course, losing speed and making leeway.

TACKING IN WAVES

Tacking in waves is all about picking your moment to turn. If, for instance, you tack as you hit a wave you will probably end up going backwards and lose many boat lengths. Time your tack so that you are putting the tiller across just as you start going down the wave. By doing this you can complete your tack before you reach the next wave. Keeping your balance is difficult, and needs lots of practice.

TACKING IN LIGHT WINDS

In the lightest of airs, say under 3 knots, it is possible to accelerate out of the tack quicker than you went into it. This, however, is illegal so extreme care should be taken in these conditions. The rule states "A yacht's crew may move their bodies to exaggerate the rolling that facilitates steering the yacht through a tack or gybe provided that, at the moment the

tack or gybe is completed, the yacht's speed is not greater than it would have been in the absence of the tack or gybe."

Conditions Zero to 6 knots of wind.

How to roll tack Assume you are on starboard tack. Prepare yourself and your crew as mentioned earlier, then bear away 5 degrees from the wind to gather more speed. Working together, heel the boat to leeward and luff at the same time. When you are back hard on the wind, call "tack". Your crew should then join you on the weather side, rolling the boat over to weather while you, at the same time, put the tiller across. Do not cross the boat until you

Roll the boat through each tack.

are past head to wind but heel the boat over to weather as far as possible without taking water over the side. As soon as the boat has turned halfway between head to wind and the new closehauled course, both of you should cross the boat smoothly and hike out together on the new side deck, bringing the boat upright. At the midpoint of the tack (as the sail flaps) ease the

Note that the tiller extension and sheet stay in the same hand until the tack is complete. Only then do you grab the tiller extension with the right hand (still holding the sheet) and finally transfer the sheet to the left hand.

mainsheet. Only pull it in again after you have started righting the boat on the new tack. Tacking in this way has the effect of `wafting' the whole rig through as large an arc as possible, forcing air over the sails and driving you forward.

TACKING IN HEAVY WINDS

Conditions Sixteen to 28 knots of wind.

Technique Assume you are on starboard tack. Tell your crew that you wish to tack

Roll tacking. This is
an essential
manoeuvre when
racing in light airs.

and will be doing so on the next suitable
wave. You can then wait and look for the
smallest wave. As the boat reaches the
crest of the wave *before* the one you have
picked, call your crew; he can then come in
off the trapeze and be ready to tack. Point
the boat closer to the wind as he comes in

and uncleat both main and jib sheets. As
the boat begins to accelerate down your
chosen wave put the helm over and cross
the boat. As soon as you are on the new
tack your crew must be out on his trapeze,
with you in complete control before you
reach the top of the next wave.

4 THE WEATHER MARK

ROUNDING THE WEATHER MARK ONTO A REACH

Before approaching the mark talk through what you're going to do. First, check your compass bearing so you can determine if the reach is going to be close or broad. Then, assuming you're trapezing:

1 The helmsman uncleats the sheet and guy.

2 The next job is to set the guy. If you have a stopper knot the crew needs to bend his legs and pull the guy aft (so the kite comes partly out of the bag).

3 The helmsman now sets the windward twinning line, or puts the guy into the reaching hook at the correct mark.

If the wind is too light for trapezing approach the mark on starboard so your crew can partially set the spinnaker pole before you reach the mark, making for a faster set.

If the wind is stronger it can pay to pass the (telescopic) tiller extension and the mainsheet to your crew and then go forward yourself to partially set the pole. This manoeuvre depends largely on your position relative to other boats.

Starboard tack approach Usually it pays to approach the mark on starboard so that you can set the pole as mentioned already and also so that you have right of way over port-tack boats going into the mark. If you have worked out that the wind has backed (making the reach very close) it will pay you to over-stand, providing you are not in the first ten coming in to the mark. This is because you can then come into the mark at top speed and stay up to weather of other boats once rounded. Having done this your

Rounding the weather mark onto a reach.

A windward hoist from bags.

options are open once you get further down the reach - you can either go high and hoist the spinnaker later or you can bear away and aim straight for the mark. In either case, because the reach is close, you will have gained as your speed will be as good as boats to leeward.

If, however, the wind has veered, then try not to overstand the windward mark as you will probably want to stay down to leeward on the forthcoming reach. To do this you have to be on the inside when rounding the mark so that you can then steer straight without being luffed by boats inside you.

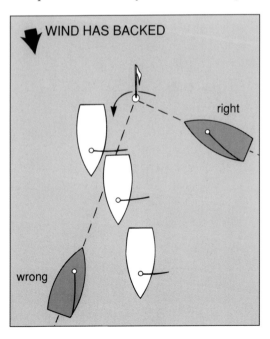

WIND HAS BACKED

right

wrong

Port tack approach The port tack into the mark will only pay if:

1 You are well separated from the rest of the fleet and boats reaching down from the weather mark are not going to take your wind as you beat up.

2 The fleet is well spread out and you are confident about finding a gap to tack into between boats approaching on starboard.

The port tack is sometimes effective if boats on starboard are queueing up to go round the mark as they will all be overstanding trying to keep their air clear. It is a manoeuvre that should be treated with great caution, but can gain several places especially in non-spinnaker boats.

The rounding Before you reach the mark, ease the vang, cunningham and outhaul to their correct reaching positions. As soon as your stern clears the mark bear away onto your chosen course and ease the main and jibsheets. Now come in from the side deck, stand in the centre of the boat, cleat the mainsheet and hoist the spinnaker, steering with the tiller between your knees. At the same time the crew pushes out the pole and clips it onto the mast. Once he has hoisted, the helmsman pulls in the spinnaker sheet and hands it to the crew.

As the crew goes out on the wire, the spinnaker fills. Having the helmsman tend the sheet also stops the sheet going over the boom. In a perfect hoist the spinnaker should never flap.

When the crew is out on the trapeze with the spinnaker full and pulling, you can adjust the mainsail and jib for maximum drive, raise the centreboard and begin steering your best course to the gybe mark.

ROUNDING THE WEATHER MARK ONTO A RUN

It is vital to know the true wind direction before you reach the mark as this will tell you which gybe to be on after the rounding. If you are well down the fleet, it will also tell you which tack to be on approaching the mark. For example, if you know the wind has backed you will also know that the fleet will be coming down the run on the starboard gybe and it will, therefore, pay to avoid them by approaching on starboard tack. The opposite is true if the wind has veered.

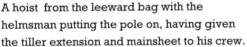

A hoist from the leeward bag with the helmsman putting the pole on, having given the tiller extension and mainsheet to his crew.

The rounding Unless the wind has veered more than 10 degrees it will pay to hoist the spinnaker on the starboard gybe and then either stay on starboard or gybe onto port once it is set. By doing this you will be able to carry your way round the mark and make a faster spinnaker hoist. Set the pole if possible before reaching the mark, ease vang and cunningham as before, and as soon as you have cleared the buoy let the mainsheet go so the mainsail goes out all the way and stops against the shroud; there is no need to waste time cleating the sheet. Hoist the spinnaker as quickly as possible while your crew cleats the guy. Finally pass him the sheet before you sit down on the leeward side.

If the wind has veered more than 10 degrees you have to gybe at the weather mark and will consequently not have set the pole. If this is the case, then ease vang and cunningham before the rounding and gybe onto port as close to the mark as possible, heeling the boat to windward and easing the sails to help bear away without using too much rudder. Turning close prevents any boats getting inside you and on your wind. As soon as your gybe is complete and both sheets have been eased, your crew can put the pole out while you hoist the spinnaker. As you will have hoisted before your crew has finished pushing the pole out, it is up to you to fill the spinnaker. Do this by standing up and steering with the tiller between your knees. If the guy cleats are behind the shroud, set the guy and then trim the sheet. Once the pole is on the mast, hand the sheet to your crew who can then coax the spinnaker round to windward.

5 REACHING

REACHING IN MEDIUM WINDS

Conditions Six to 15 knots of wind.

The rig Good reaching speed is mainly due to correct hull and spinnaker shape. To be competitive your boat must have both; you must also, however, pay attention to the following points.

1 Mainsail If you are using a flat main then everything possible must be done to create more fullness in the sail. Ease the outhaul 3 to 4 inches - most sails are now made with a 'lens foot' which creates more depth in the sail when the outhaul is released and helps downwind speed enormously. Ease both shrouds if possible - this reduces rig tension and straightens the mast creating more fullness in the sail. Better still, ease the leeward shroud. The windward spreader now pushes the middle of the mast to leeward, powering up the main. Ease the vang, and let the cunningham right off.

2 Jib Release the cunningham and barber haul the sheet lead forward to stop the top of the sail twisting too far off and becoming inefficient.

3 Spinnaker Set the spinnaker pole so that both clews are parallel with the boat. If the pole is too high the weather clew of the sail will be higher than the leeward, and vice versa if the pole is too low. Raise the pole height in stronger winds and lower it in lighter winds to produce maximum efficiency from the kite. Make sure your sheet leads are as far back as you can get them in order to keep the leech as open and as far away from the mainsail as possible. Check that your sheets and halyard are non-stretch and of minimum diameter.

The spinnaker guy should be cleated level with the shroud, helping to keep the pole from 'skying' and also reducing the amount of sheet liable to stretch between

This helmsman's toestraps can be loosened for beating and tightened for reaching.

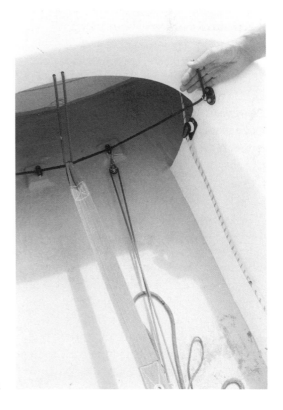

Pole too high, choking the slot between main and spinnaker.

Correct (note the clews are level).

clew and cleat. When the wind is forward of the beam set the pole 1 inch off the forestay; don't let it touch or you will run the

This cutaway boom allows the boat to heel further before the boom hits the water.

risk of breaking the pole and wearing a hole in the jib luff (a sign of bad crewing!). Never cleat the spinnaker sheet but constantly play it as the wind direction changes, easing the sheet until the luff is just `breaking'. As speed increases the spinnaker needs to be sheeted in harder due to the apparent wind moving forward. Play the mainsheet in the same way with the luff of the sail just beginning to break.

Boat trim Providing the class of boat you sail is well balanced, it always pays to keep the boat level. But in classes like the 505 which has a long spinnaker pole the boat develops lee helm, forcing you to sail with up to 15 degrees of heel to keep it going in a straight line. Helmsman and crew should be as close together as possible and move forward together on top of any wave to help

Pole too low, causing the luff of the spinnaker to be too round, making trimming impossible.

With the pole too low the leech is open which may help you get up to a buoy.

the boat down the far side and, once surfing, move back aft to stop the bow burying in the trough.

Centreboard Raise the centreboard enough to stop the boat slipping sideways; in most cases half the area down would be correct.

Steering Make sure your rudder is vertical – if it isn't the helm will be heavy and control not 100 per cent.

If there are no other boats around you a straight line course to the mark is usually the best. In marginal planing conditions huge gains can be made by keeping the boat planing: bear away as much as possible in the gusts, while keeping the boat planing. In a lull luff as little as possible to keep her on the plane. Naturally, the

helmsman and crew must synchronise sail trim throughout.

It is important always to keep an eye on the wind to weather and ahead, because if you spot a gust coming down towards you it may pay to luff up and get into it early, then bear away back on course with greater speed. If, however, you see that the wind is dropping light it will pay to bear away, so that you can luff up when you hit less wind and keep your speed up.

If the reach is too close to set your spinnaker, it can pay to luff up to 10 degrees above the course to the mark and sail three-quarters of the reach before bearing away for the mark and hoisting the spinnaker. By doing this you sail a greater distance but more than make up for it in speed. You will also get to windward of the pack and maybe able to roll them.

Lower the pole if you are struggling to get up to the buoy. If you still can't lay it partially drop the spinnaker to close reach (or beat) up to the mark. Finally, hoist the spinnaker again if time allows.

REACHING IN LIGHT WINDS

Conditions Zero to 6 knots of wind.

The rig In the lightest of winds never create too much fullness in the mainsail as it will tend to stall. Ease the outhaul 1 inch, check the cunningham is off and ease the vang until there is sufficient twist to make the top telltale just begin to flow. Ease the jib cunningham and barber haul the sheet lead out and forward. Lower the spinnaker pole to keep the clews level and the sail pulling properly. If the reach becomes very close, pull the traveller to weather to

Hold the jib out on the reach to prevent excessive twist.

retain sufficient twist in the sail.

Boat trim In these conditions both helmsman and crew should be seated well forward, the crew up against the shroud on the weather side and the helmsman in front of the traveller down to leeward. It is the helmsman's job to balance the boat and in gusts and lulls he should be moving in or outboard, leaving the crew to focus all his attention on setting the spinnaker. If there is a sudden gust, the helmsman should move onto the weather side, positioning himself either on the deck or inboard astride the traveller. Never let your crew go out on the trapeze until you are to weather of the centreline. In marginal trapezing conditions it pays to let your crew stay out on the trapeze while you balance the boat, moving from the side deck to the centreline.

Centreboard Raise the centreboard enough to stop sideways `slip' - usually leaving half of the board in the water is correct.

Steering Be very gentle on the helm, making smooth and small changes in direction. If the wind drops, head up to keep speed on and the spinnaker filling, wait for a good enough gust and then carefully bear away as far as possible without collapsing the spinnaker. It is generally an advantage to steer above your course for the mark if this is the only way to keep your spinnaker filling.

REACHING IN HEAVY WINDS

Conditions Sixteen to 35 knots of wind.

The rig If you find yourself ovepowered and unable to lay the mark, then a reduction in power is required. You have the following controls to adjust.

1 The outhaul should be pulled out to the black band to flatten the lower third of the sail.

2 Pull on the pre-bender to prevent the spinnaker pole inverting the mast. Bend the mast, flattening the main and opening the slot between the main and spinnaker.

3 Pull the cunningham down as hard as you can; this `drags' the fullness in the sail forwards, opens up the leech and bends the mast, flattening the sail even more.

4 Ease the vang progressively until the mainsail is twisted with the top completely open, spilling air out of its upper half. Easing the vang is your only way of spilling the wind out of the mainsail as the spinnaker sheet prevents the boom from moving further outboard than the line between fairlead and clew.

5 If you're still overpowered, raise the centreboard more.

Never oversheet the jib, and in extreme conditions ease it out until the front half of the sail is lifting, thereby dumping more power. Always keep the spinnaker pole

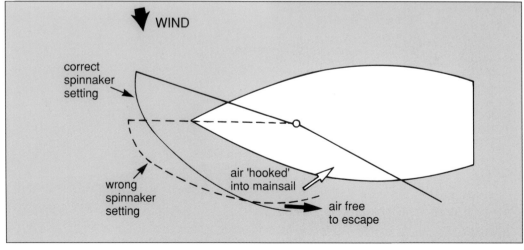

two inches off the forestay so that the leech of the spinnaker doesn't `hook' air back into the mainsail (see diagram on page 45).

If you really can't lay the gybe mark the helmsman releases the spinnaker halyard while the crew, still on the wire, pulls the sheet tight. The reach is completed with the kite flapping in the lee of the mainsail. Sail high then bear away, hoist, trim the kite and gybe round the mark.

Boat trim Position yourselves as close together as possible with your crew's feet either side of the traveller. As you surf down a wave you will both have to move aft to stop the bow burying into the trough. Do not, however, move aft too far or you will dig the stern in the water and raise the bow too far out, creating more windage. Sail the boat level and make sure your crew is as low on his trapeze adjusters as possible. He should be just skimming the wave tops with neither his legs nor his back bent. To do this he will have to play the sheet with one hand - it is not possible to use both hands because the trapeze wire is in the way. You should be hiking as far out as you can get, lying flat so that you don't drag your body through the waves.

Centreboard Raise the centreboard until you can feel the boat just begin to slide to leeward: one-third of its area is usually sufficient.

Steering Luff up in the lulls and bear away in the gusts. In waves you must always be looking ahead for a suitable wave to surf down. As the waves will normally be running across your course you must bear away onto each one to promote surfing; once you are surfing head up, thereby prolonging the effective length of the wave by steering diagonally along it.

Once you reach the trough again head up to keep your bow out of the back of the next wave, and then sail over this wave and bear away down its face. As you surf down the face your speed will increase dramatically and you will have to sheet in rapidly due to the apparent wind moving forward.

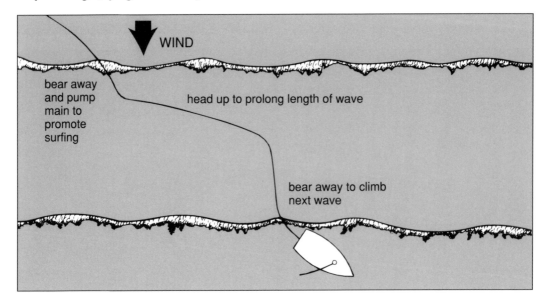

WIND

bear away and pump main to promote surfing

head up to prolong length of wave

bear away to climb next wave

6 THE GYBE MARK

It is the exit from the gybe mark rather than the approach that is all-important. Always aim to be on the inside of any group of boats and plan your approach down the reach with that in mind. If you do have to give water to another boat you may lose more than one place as other boats can slip in between you and the mark. If another boat does have an overlap, always point the boat directly at the mark and then luff at the last moment before reaching the two boat-lengths circle. This will usually enable you to accelerate away, breaking the overlap. If you are trying to establish an overlap, stay four to five lengths down to leeward of the opposition and reach up to the buoy at the last moment, coming in to the mark at greater speed. But don't luff too soon or you will end up in their windshadow.

GYBING IN MEDIUM WINDS

Preparation before you reach the gybe mark is all-important. You must go through the following procedure, whatever your position relative to other boats.

Approximately ten lengths before the mark, cleat the spinnaker guy on the side tank. Then cleat the weather jib sheet, pulling 6 to 9 inches of the jib's clew to weather. Cleat the mainsail in its correct position for the next reach.

When you are two lengths from the mark, uncleat the old jib sheet so the sail is set for the next reach; tell your crew to come in off the trapeze and pull on the new twinning line. During the gybe the crew throws the boom over and releases the old twinning line. Meanwhile you pull the old guy hard, swinging the spinnaker round behind the main on the new side, keeping it full. The crew now does the pole while you trim the sheet, then hand it to him.

Steering Always, if possible approach the mark from above the straight line course. This enables you to bear away onto a broad reach as you approach the last four lengths of the leg, thereby enabling your crew to come in off the trapeze, to unhook himself and get ready for the gybe. It also means that you can do a smoother and more controlled gybe as your boat will be gybing through a smaller angle. In some cases it is possible to complete your gybe before you reach the mark by sailing the last few lengths on a run, and gybing while still running. This is particularly effective when the second reach is very close, in that it enables you to steer immediately for the next mark, without giving away distance to leeward while completing the gybe.

Vang and centreboard As you approach the mark, make sure your vang is well eased, as this raises the boom, reducing the chances of it hitting the water immediately after gybing. It also reduces pressure on the mainsail due to the wind escaping out of the top. Make sure the centreboard is approximately halfway down as too much will cause the boat to 'trip over' itself, and too little will make the boat unstable. The friction device on the centreboard must hold it firmly in position.

Rounding the gybe mark. The crew comes in off the trapeze, uncleats the guy from the reaching hook and pulls the jib round. The helmsman begins to pull the boom over.

The crew takes the pole off the mast and clips it on to the new guy before pushing the pole out and clipping the end on to the mast. The crew pulls the guy

At the same time the crew begins to pull the guy around to windward. Then he puts the new guy under the reaching hook. The helm reverses the tiller as the boom comes over.

around to its mark while the helmsman pulls in the spinaker sheet. The helmsman passes the sheet to the crew who hooks on to the trapeze.

A roll gybe

Timing Always gybe when the boat is going at full speed as this is when there is the least pressure on the sails. If you are accelerating or slowing down, the pressure on the sails is obviously greater. You can experience this when surfing down steep waves - on occasions your boom will `drift' towards the centreline of the boat of its own accord, due to the boat going faster than the wind. Therefore whenever possible, gybe going down a wave, never in a trough or riding up a wave.

Once you have begun to gybe, never change your mind as this will nearly always end in a capsize. Begin your turn by slowly bearing away until you are running dead downwind. Once you have reached this point, pull the tiller a little harder, give a good pull on the mainsheet to bring the

boom over, and then cross the boat. Your mainsheet is cleated so you only have to worry about your tiller. As soon as the boom has crossed the centreline, correct your turning moment with a sharp pull the other way on the tiller. This effectively 'kills' the boat's turning momentum and gets you on a straight course for the mark.

GYBING IN LIGHT WINDS

When gybing in light winds it is most important to sail the shortest possible course around the mark without either slowing the boat or collapsing the spinnaker. To do this a great deal of co-ordination is required between helmsman and crew. Your crew will not be trapezing and should be playing both sheet and guy without using any cleats. With two lengths to go to the mark you should take the spinnaker sheet and guy from him, stand in the middle of the boat and steer with the tiller between your knees leaving your hands free to trim the spinnaker. It is the crew's job to pull the boom across and balance the boat. As the helmsman steers

the boat through the gybe the crew moves to the (old) windward side, rolling the boat and helping the boom across. Remember that in light winds the speed of the whole operation is irrelevant and the speed and direction of the boat all-important. The crew should, therefore, be careful not to collapse the spinnaker when switching the pole over from one gybe to the other.

Steering Approaching the mark, aim to be one length to weather of it with two lengths to go. This enables you to bear away slowly, while at the same time 'squaring' the pole around without collapsing the spinnaker. Any boats behind cannot overtake you immediately after the gybe by doing a tighter turn or by heading up above you after the gybe, because they will slow down in doing this. So you can sail this course regardless of other competitors.

Vang and centreboard Leave the centreboard three quarters down or even fully down to help squirt the boat forward as you roll. A little vang tension will help the top batten flip over and prevent the boom coming off the gooseneck.

Non-spinnaker roll gybes Lower the centreboard fully and pull on the vang a little. The crew now rolls the boat to windward. The boom will naturally come over as the boat is steered through the gybe. As the boom kisses the water pause, let the mainsail fill, then pull the boat upright smoothly and accelerate forwards. Finally, readjust the centreboard and vang.

GYBING IN HEAVY WINDS

If the wind is less than 28 knots a good gybe with a spinnaker is possible. In winds over 28 knots it is better simply to get around the mark, regardless of speed, and stay upright!

As mentioned previously, the only time to gybe is when going at maximum speed and, in strong winds, if you do try to gybe at any other time you will almost certainly capsize. No matter how good a helmsman you are, 28 knots of wind hitting a boat going, say, 3 knots, will strike with tremendous force. Therefore get your boat speed as near to the wind speed as possible before you gybe.

Steering You must approach the mark from well to windward so that your crew can come in off the trapeze to unhook himself and the spinnaker guy, and pull on the new twinning line (so both are on). By giving yourself weather room you have time to prepare and can pick your moment to gybe. The helmsman has the tiller in one hand and the sheet (straight from the boom)

Left: **During a run-to-run gybe steer with your knees, cleat the main and play the spinnaker sheet and guy while the crew sets the pole.** *Opposite:* **Whenever possible gybe going down a wave to reduce the pressure on the sail.**

in the other. The crew is concentrating hard on keeping the kite full, maximising boatspeed. Now take a breath, bear away firmly and flick the boom across. The crew stays central, waiting to balance if necessary. Once the danger is over, complete the manoeuvre as usual.

Vang and sheets Before you gybe, make sure the vang is on firmly. Cleat the mainsheet at the broad reach setting and leave it there throughout the gybe. In extreme conditions let off the vang after the gybe or you will have to bear off too much

while the crew sorts the pole.

Non-spinnaker heavy air gybes The problem is maximising speed as you gybe, because you have no spinnaker. However, without a kite you can (and must) gybe fast. So, maximise speed on a broad reach, pick your moment, bear away fast, gybe immediately (the crew may help the boom to flick over), steer rapidly onto the new course, hike and (this is vital) quickly trim both sails to accelerate out of the gybe. The whole effect is like a windsurfer carve gybing.

7 THE LEEWARD MARK

As you approach the leeward mark you must be aware of any changes in wind direction as they can help you in deciding which way you go up the next beat. If, for example, the reach has gradually become broader as you approach the mark, there may well be a wind bend and if so, it would pay you to hold on the port tack rather than tacking away after you have rounded the mark (as in the diagram).

In all cases plan your strategy for the beat before you round the mark. Providing no other boats are taking your wind or trying to gain an overlap on you, the best approach to the mark in light and medium winds is to stay half a length to leeward of the rhumb line so that when you drop the spinnaker you can come in to the buoy reaching at full speed. In strong winds you will need to be a couple of lengths to windward of the rhumb line so you can bear away and drop the kite.

ROUNDING WITH A SPINNAKER CHUTE

Approach the mark with ten lengths to go, put your centreboard down ready for the beat, then pull the cunningham, vang and outhaul to their marks. With your crew still on the trapeze, move into the centre of the boat, steer with your knees, uncleat the halyard and pull the spinnaker into the chute. Your crew should balance the boat

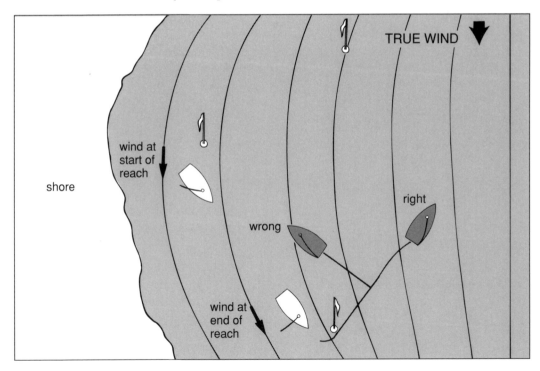

TRUE WIND

wind at start of reach

shore

right

wrong

wind at end of reach

and ease both guy and sheet before coming in off the trapeze to take the pole down.

ROUNDING WITHOUT A SPINNAKER CHUTE

Arrange your course so that you can bear away when your crew needs to come in off the trapeze. Essentially this means approaching the mark one boat length higher than with a spinnaker chute. With fifteen lengths to go, put the centreboard down and pull in vang, cunningham and outhaul. With ten lengths to go, take the spinnaker sheet from your crew and tell

him to come in off the trapeze and take the spinnaker down. As he takes the pole off the mast you can keep the spinnaker pulling as you still have a hold of the sheet. He then gathers in the foot of the sail and you uncleat the halyard, easing it off along with the sheet and making sure your don't drop the sail faster than he can stow it in its bag. You also need to tidy the guy while the crew is stowing the kite - the sheet takes care of itself. With the sail stowed away the crew can then go back out on his trapeze and you can sheet in and round the mark. Then check your controls and tidy loose sheets if necessary.

1

2

3

7

8

9

13

14

15

4

5

6

10

11

12

16

17

Rounding the leeward mark. The helmsman lowers the centreboard, and tightens the outhaul. The crew takes down the spinnaker pole. The helmsman uncleats the spinnaker halyard, steering with his knees, while the spinnaker is pulled down. The spinnaker is stowed and the vang and cunningham set up for the beat in time to allow you to concentrate on a good rounding.

8 RUNNING

RUNNING IN MEDIUM WINDS

You can gain or lose more distance on the run than on any other leg of the course. It is, therefore, important to know how to achieve good boatspeed and how to make use of any changes in the wind.

Conditions Six to 15 knots of wind.

The rig Ease both shrouds off to bring the mast more upright in the boat. This increases the effective sail area by adding height to the rig. The balance of the boat will not change whatever the mast rake, so it is obviously an advantage to keep the mast upright. Let the boom right out to the shroud (no stopper knots in the mainsheet). Unfortunately there is no way of getting maximum projected area for the bottom half of the sail. But by letting off the vang you can twist the top half so it is at right angles to the breeze. (In strong winds use more vang than this to prevent rolling.)

If you are sailing with the wind dead astern, pull the outhaul out to its black band to increase projected sail area. Raise the centreboard as far as possible without making the boat unstable.

Cleat the jib in its position for broad reaching so that if the wind shifts abeam the jib will be set to its correct trim.

The spinnaker pole should be just forward of a line through the boom (left). Pulling it too far back (centre) creates a shelf at the foot of the sail which prevents the air from escaping; but if the pole is too far forward (right) you lose projected area.

Adjust the spinnaker pole height, keeping both clews level and, normally, never bring the pole aft of a continuation line of the boom. Always remember to fly the spinnaker a good distance away from the jib luff. Never pull the pole back so far back as to choke the sail, which will prevent air flowing out of its foot. Also never let the pole go too far forward because you would lose projected area by bringing the clews too close together. Ease the cunningham on both main and jib.

Boat trim Going down the run in a spinnaker boat the helmsman should always sit to leeward and the crew to windward. This enables the crew to concentrate his full attention on trimming the spinnaker, leaving the helmsman to balance the boat, look out for waves to surf down, check the wind direction and other competitors' positions. In non-planing conditions the crew should be right up

Because the shroud prevents the boom from going square, twist the sail (right) on the run to increase projected area. A flat sail stalls the top of the main (left), while too much twist rolls the boat to weather.

against the shroud with the helmsman forward of the traveller, lifting the stern out of the water and reducing wetted surface area. The crew should be seated on the deck with his feet hooked under the toe-straps so that he can lean in or out in any gusts or lulls he detects through the pull of the spinnaker. He should also play both sheet and guy continually, with the guy running directly from the clew of the sail to his hand. By doing this he can pump the spinnaker (both sheet and guy together) - you are allowed one on each wave. The helmsman should sit on the leeward side deck holding the tiller in one hand and the mainsheet directly from the boom in the other. He can then feel any extra wind

Notice how far the centreboard is raised for running.

Slacken the leeward shroud tension to let the boom swing forward. Also, straighten the mast for maximum power

Pump the spinnaker sheet and guy, and the mainsheet. The best effect is when they are all pumped together.

Running goosewinged, with the boat heeled to weather to give neutral helm.

hitting the sail which would otherwise be undetected if the sheet had to run through a normal four-to-one purchase system.

Steering In non-planing conditions it is difficult to know your downwind tacking angle. In a Finn dinghy, for example, you can let the boom out at right angles to the boat and can, therefore, steer dead downwind. In other classes it pays to sail a series of broad reaches, tacking downwind. The angle you choose depends on speed against distance and works in the same way as when beating, in that for every degree you head up you must go significantly faster to make up for the extra distance sailed. The technique is first to reach up closer to the wind, building up more speed and moving the apparent wind forward. Then, as speed is achieved, bear away again still keeping speed on, which in turn leaves the apparent wind effectively on your quarter instead of dead astern. In gusts, again head up as the wind drops and bear away as it picks up.

Steer through the waves by reaching up to gain speed to overtake the next wave in front. As soon as the boat begins to surf bear away down the next wave and head back towards the mark. Sail by the lee so as to move diagonally along the wave and ride it as long as possible. Just before you hit the trough head up again and, with your crew, move aft to lift the bow over the next wave and on down its face.

RUNNING IN LIGHT WINDS

Conditions Zero to 6 knots of wind.

The rig Set this up as for medium winds, but make sure your spinnaker sheets are of minimum diameter.

On a light air run lower the pole to keep the spinnaker clews level.

On a light-weather run you must keep the spinnaker pulling but without sailing too much extra distance. When the spinnaker begins to collapse, head up (which brings the apparent wind forward) to fill the spinnaker; once you have regained speed bear away back on course.

Wave technique on the run. As you climb a wave head up *(left)* to help you accelerate. At the top bear away *(centre)* and pump the mainsail and the spinnaker *(right)* to promote surfing.

Boat trim Both helm and crew should sit right up against the shrouds to lift the transom and reduce wetted surface area.

Sail the boat with a slight heel to windward as this helps to keep the spinnaker filling (providing you are dead downwind with the majority of the sail over on the weather side). Hold the boom out with your hand to stop it swinging into the centre of the boat and don't worry if the sail does not appear to be filling. If you do heel the boat to leeward you will get a better-looking mainsail by making it set under its

own weight; it will not, however, be any faster as it is still projected area that is required on a run. The important factor is keeping the spinnaker filled: lowering the pole will help in very light airs.

Steering Bear away on any small gust that you get and head back up in the lulls. Always steer tó keep the spinnaker filling - this will mean constantly altering course, heading up as you see the sail begin to collapse and back down as boatspeed improves. A good understanding with your crew is necessary and he must tell you when he feels you can bear away a little and still keep the spinnaker filling, or should head up because it is beginning to collapse. In order to keep speed up in these conditions you may find you have to steer well above the rhumb line. Obviously, if you have to sail twice the distance to the leeward mark to keep the spinnaker filling, you know you must go at least twice as fast and in the lightest airs this is hard to achieve. It is usually advantageous to sail a course somewhere in between, accepting that your spinnaker will not be filling for some of the time.

RUNNING IN HEAVY WINDS

Conditions Sixteen to 35 knots of wind.

The rig Always keep a check on the twist in your mainsail as too much vang will slow you down and too little will make the boat unstable. Only ease the shrouds off in winds under 20 knots as in stronger winds the mast will need the support.

Boat trim If the wind is strong but under 28 knots the helmsman should sit on the leeward side deck behind the traveller. The crew is to weather but further aft than in medium conditions. Use your weight in waves: if you are sailing down long rollers, for example, you should sit with your legs either side of the traveller and slide your weight forward to help the boat down the face, then back again before you get to the trough. If the wind is over 28 knots you must still fly the spinnaker but with the helmsman to weather and the crew to leeward. The crew should cleat the spinnaker guy and play the sheet as he would a jib in a non-spinnaker boat - by doing this he is free to move around and balance the boat. Meanwhile the helmsman concentrates on steering the boat through the waves and, being to weather, is in a better position to see dangerous waves and gusts approaching.

Centreboard Leave half the centreboard down - any less may result in the boat rolling and becoming unstable.

Steering In strong winds the boat will be travelling at near her maximum speed so a straight-line course to the mark is best because it is shortest. In flat water this is no problem because you should be able to make the mark on one gybe. In certain classes, eg 505, it pays in waves to do two reaches, with the crew on the trapeze and the helmsman to windward. This keeps the boat planing while others are sailing slower and hitting the waves. The technique here is as for medium winds; surf down each wave and, as your bow reaches the bottom, luff up and swing the boat at an angle to the back of the next wave. When doing this in strong winds it is vital that you don't bury the bow and slow down, because if this happens pressure on the sails will increase dramatically and you will run the risk of either capsizing or losing your mast over the bows.

9 CAPSIZING

Even Olympic sailors capsize. Since it's going to happen to you sometime, it's worth thinking about how you're going to recover, fast.

Boat considerations

It makes sense to tie everything into the boat. There's nothing worse than having to swim after your gear in the middle of a capsize. Make a bag to carry the halyard tails, or they'll end up tangled round everything.

Always carry a bailer and sponge so if you capsize in light airs you can empty the boat.

Think carefully about your bailers. Small bailers suck at lower speeds than large ones: Ian's 505 has a small bailer well forward for light airs, and a large one aft for heavy winds. Most bailers have sharp edges: after capsizing, shut the bailer before righting. We've seen some nasty accidents where people fell on an open bailer.

If your class rules permit, fit transom flaps: they are the quickest way of getting rid of water. Another trick when sailing is to steer the boat sharply one way, then the other. Sometimes the water will hit the tanks and slop over the rear quarter.

Preventing capsizes on a heavy air beat

There are four common causes of capsizing on a beat.

● **Ducking transoms** Make sure you ease both sheets and keep the boat flat, or the boom will hit the water and pitch you in.

● **Large squalls** Again, ease both sheets.

● **Tacking** Invest in the best jib cleats. Consider fitting vertical fairleads, especially in boats which have heavily loaded jibsheets.

● **Crash tacking** Keep a good lookout for other boats and don't be forced into a sudden tack.

Preventing capsizes on a heavy air reach

● Cut away the end of the boom to help prevent its hitting the water.

● Consider a flattening reef system in the clew of the main. When this is wound on, the shape is taken out of the foot, and the boom is raised.

● Play the mainsheet all the time to keep the boat flat.

● Ease the vang when hoisting and lowering the kite.

● Make sure there is no play in the rudder, which should preferably be fixed.

● Use the crew weight sensibly.

● Keep the boat moving fast. In a real squall, bear away - and just go faster. In the next lull, take down the kite.

Preventing capsizes on a heavy air run

● Put on lots of vang tension.

● Avoid sailing by the lee, which will make you roll.

● Keep crew weight back, to prevent nosediving.

● In a real howler, head up a bit so both helmsman and crew can sit to windward.

● Pin the spinnaker down hard by pulling on both twinning lines. Try to keep the spinnaker close to the boat to stop it oscillating.

Preventing capsizes when gybing

● Gybe quickly, and at full speed.

● Pull on some vang before you gybe.

● Make sure there is no slop in the rudder.

● As the boom hits the new shroud, reverse the rudder to stop the boat broaching.

Capsizing with the spinnaker up

Avoid going upside down at all costs - it will then take five times as long to right the boat. So as you capsize go for the centreboard and try to keep the boat on her side. In any case, don't hang on to the inside of the hull, which always causes the boat to invert. You can have a go at righting with the kite up if

it's not too windy and you have capsized to leeward. However if it's very windy or you've capsized to windward, you'll have to pull down the spinnaker before you can right the boat. Get the boat on its side, position the crew on the centreboard, then swim into the boat, release the halyard and sheet and guy, move forward to the mast and pull as much as possible of the kite down into the bag.

Righting the boat

Before trying to right the boat make sure the main and jibsheets are uncleated and

The crew goes for the centreboard to stop the boat inverting. The helmsman swims round and drops the kite, before going to the bow to help swing the hull into the wind. Finally, he clambers in over the transom.

the vang is off. Most modern boats swing round rapidly until the hull is downwind of the mast. To right from this position try the RYA training method: one person lies in the water inside the boat (but not holding it down) while the other does his stuff on the centreboard. As the boat comes up it

scoops in the man in the water and his weight may stop it flipping over the other way.

Alternatively, one person gets in the water and swims the bow round so the boat is head to wind. The other person can then pull the boat upright.

Upside down

You will need to have both people standing on one gunwale, levering on the centreboard, to get the boat on her side. Alternatively, throw a sheet over and pull on that, uncleating it as the boat comes up.

10 TWIN-WIRING

Having both helmsman and crew on trapezes is the only way to fly!

Getting the boat right

Make sure the tiller extension is long enough.

You need a good centre mainsheet

system with an effective jammer. Attach the tail of the mainsheet to the centreline with a thin piece of elastic, or the mainsheet will forever be trailing in the water.

Lead the vang to each gunwale, where the helmsman can reach it. Lead the other controls to the shroud area so the crew can reach them.

As helmsman, your trapeze has no handles (you'll have the mainsheet in one hand and the tiller in the other). Set the trapeze a little higher than normal, so you have to raise your hips a bit to clip on. Once out, trapeze higher than your crew so you can see over him.

Make sure the gunwales are non-slip, and fit toe loops on short boats (where you need to be well back to prevent the bow burying).

Technique

Hold the tiller by your side as though you were holding a sword. Hold the mainsheet in the other hand; to pull in, transfer rope to your tiller hand across your body and in front of the trapeze wire.

Who trapezes?

Beating in light airs Sail as you would in a conventional boat, with the helmsman on the gunwale and the crew trapezing if necessary to keep the boat flat.

On the Laser 5000 the mainsheet is attached to the tail of the vang, and the cunningham is attached to the jibsheet.

In light airs the helmsman stays in the boat.

In medium winds the helmsman stays on the wire while the crew moves to balance the boat.

Beating in medium airs The helmsman stays out on the wire and concentrates on sailing the boat, while the crew moves in and out as required.

Beating in heavy air Obviously you will both be trapezing.

Tacking

● Warn your crew that you plan to tack.

● Now come in a little before him.

● Ease the main a bit and cleat it.

● Unhook using your mainsheet hand.

● Cross the boat facing forward and swing the tiller extension round the back of the boat, still keeping hold of the base of it.

● Change hands on the tiller extension.

● Clip on.

● Grab the mainsheet.

● Go out.

In strong winds you will both be trapezing.

Reaching

For a spinnaker hoist let the vang off first. Then both of you come into the boat for the hoist. Once the kite is up the helmsman goes out on the wire, trimming the main. Finally the crew goes out, filling the kite as he does so.

For a gybe the helmsman comes in slightly earlier. After the gybe you can race each other out onto the wires.

For a spinnaker drop the helmsman stays on the wire while the crew comes in and drops the pole and kite.

Twin-wire tacking on a Laser 5000. Come in, unhook, turn the boat while facing forwards and pushing the tiller extension round aft. Transfer the mainsheet to your aft (tiller) hand. Hook on, then step onto the gunwale and finally onto the rack.

After a capsize let off the vang and use all your weight to right the boat.

11 ASYMMETRICS

Asymmetrics are fast and fun. For crash and burn thrills and spills racing, they're great.

Boat and gear

The asymmetric spinnaker is rather like a large genoa made from lightweight spinnaker cloth which is flown from a retractable tapered carbon fibre bowsprit. This protrudes about 10 feet - so the masthead kite can be huge. The sail is sheeted with fairleads at the back of the

The asymmetric tends to make the boat bear away, so let her heel a little until the helm is neutral.

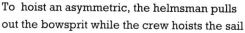

To hoist an asymmetric, the helmsman pulls out the bowsprit while the crew hoists the sail

boat and tweakers can be fitted further forward (similar to twinning lines), so that the sail can be made more powerful for broad reaches.

These rigs have high loads so slightly stronger gear is required; cap shrouds are fitted to help support the mast above the hounds, and deck control is vital to stop the mast from inverting.

Hoisting

Both helmsman and crew come in. The helmsman pulls out the bowsprit while the crew hoists the spinnaker. Finally the helmsman pulls the spinnaker sheet to take up the slack, ready to pass it to the crew.

Setting on a reach

Set the jib for a reach. The crew then concentrates on the luff of the spinnaker, sheeting out constantly to keep the luff on the verge of curling. However, when

struggling to lay a mark in heavy air dump more sheet so the leading two feet of the sail curls: you have effectively reduced sail area. The boat will slow, bringing the apparent wind aft, which allows you to head up.

Running

You don't run with an asymmetric: sail downwind in a series of broad reaches. The aim is to maximise VMG by sailing as low as possible while keeping the boat planing. You will normally have at least one person on the wire. The key to getting downhill fast is windspeed - go wherever the pressure is greatest. The difference in boatspeed from a couple of knots more wind is dramatic. It's on the downwind legs that most place changing occurs. If you need more power, pull on the leeward tweaker to put more draft into the sail.

The asymmetric produces lee helm. To counteract this heel the boat up to 15 degrees to leeward. And don't steer close to windward of boats or obstructions: you will automatically bear away in gusts.

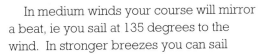

In medium winds your course will mirror a beat, ie you sail at 135 degrees to the wind. In stronger breezes you can sail more downwind. In light winds it pays to head up a little if you can plane; if not, sail deep.

Gybing is simplicity itself because an asymmetric is just like a big jib.

Gybing

If possible, furl the jib as this gives the asymmetric more stable air and makes gybing easier. You lose a lot each time you gybe, so keep the number to a minimum. But of course, you will need to gybe on major shifts and to move across the course looking for higher pressure.

To gybe:

● Both helm and crew come in together.

● Turn sharply and throw the boom across.

● At the same time the crew pulls the asymmetric round to the new side. Three quick arm lengths and the sail is there.

● Turn onto a higher course initially to help the asymmetric set and build boatspeed. Then bear away onto your normal course for maximum VMG.

The Drop

● Bear away a little and ease the mainsheet a bit to keep the boat flat. The helmsman can stay comfortably on the wire while the crew does all the work!

● He unfurls the genoa first.

● He uncleats the halyard and pulls on the retrieval line until the foot of the sail goes tight.

● He then uncleats the retractable bowsprit line, and retrieves the remainder of the spinnaker.

PART 2

THE RACE

12 PREPARATION

Before any regatta begins you must prepare yourself and the boat. On arriving at the venue do not stroll around the dinghy park examining other boats; you will have plenty of time to do this during the regatta, and it may raise doubts in your mind about the quality of your own boat in comparison to later fancy models. Concentrate instead on your own boat and either work on it or stay away from the park. Make sure you have done any major work to your boat before you arrive - last minute sanding of boards and rudders should be avoided as it will take your mind off more important matters.

If possible, try to arrive a few days before the championship to acclimatise and familiarise yourself with the surroundings. Go out and sail three or four hours a day to get used to the wave and wind patterns. You can usually pick up local shifts and tide effects and generally get a better feeling for the course you will compete on. Check out the tide on the course; get hold of a chart of the area and write down times and directions of flow so that you can transfer them to your boat prior to each race.

Unless you are allowed several suits of sails in a series, decide well in advance which ones you are going to have

measured, as last-minute decisions will only divert your line of thought away from the race itself. Never choose sails that perform only in certain conditions (conditions seldom remain constant for a full week), but pick the sails that will be good in all conditions.

If possible have back-up sails, identical sails to the ones you are using, and make sure they *are* identical before you arrive at the venue. If you don't have these and tear a sail you are unlikely to perform as well with your second choice, if only for psychological reasons.

Before the race

Arrive at the boat park three hours before the start, check the weather forecast and go and rig your boat, using your tuning sheet to get the settings right. Pay particular attention to the spreaders and make sure all shackles, split pins, etc. are in order, and prepare for launching. Get changed and make another check of the weather forecast. Unless you are convinced the wind will be light always take your weight jacket out in a polythene bag. You can then either soak the weight jacket or leave it dry in the bag. If water bottles are allowed take them out full - if the wind stays light simply dump the water from the bottles before the five-minute gun.

Make sure you know the sailing instructions and check the notice board for any changes. Be on the water so that you are in the race area with 45 minutes to the start. Remember to take out plenty of fluid and also some chocolate or glucose.

Tides

Unless you are sailing on a small inland water, tides and currents always play a major part in championship strategy.

Before any series begins you must have access to good charts of the area. If you have these you can gain most of the information you need before you even arrive.

You can also familiarise yourself with the surrounding land and generally get to know more about the course you are preparing to sail on.

Once you have a chart, make out your own list of water speeds and directions, something like this:

Hours to high water	water speed (knots)	direction
6	1.0	020
5	1.5	035
4	2.0	040
3	2.0	045
2	1.5	050
1	0.5	050

You can then stick this to your boat (covering it with see-through plastic) for use in every race. For example, if your start is at 3:00 pm and high water is 6:00 pm you will know that the tide is running in a direction of 045 at 2.00 knots at your start. You can then work out that on your last beat the flow will have moved to 050 and reduced to 0.5 knots in speed. This should give you an advantage over most of your rivals who will only know speed and direction of the tide at the start of the race.

Checking tides on days before the race is also useful, but usually the chart gives the best information. However, always look out for local effects when you are sailing close to the shore, and remember that the tide turns first inshore.

Using the tide

Always be careful on the start line when

there is a lot of tide. If it is still running with you it will pay to hold back behind the line and come in fast and late whilst other boats are reaching along the line trying to stay behind it.

If the flow is against you beware of being late across the line, and in light airs, providing there is no one-minute rule, it invariably pays to stay above the line, dipping back behind it 15 seconds before the gun. This manoeuvre may sound risky, but you are in a position of having greater speed than boats to leeward and, therefore, can pick your spot along the line when you see a gap.

If the tide is along the line it makes the start difficult to judge. For example, if the tide is running right to left and it is a port-end start, make sure you are not too early. Most sailors underestimate the strength of the tide and, with careful calculation, you should always be able to capitalise on a strong tide and make a good start at either end.

On the beat always try to get the flow on your lee bow. Whatever you have read about this theory, believe us, it pays. It is even worth pointing a little high and losing speed if it means your switching the flow from your weather bow to your lee bow.

Forming a race plan

Having left the beach, usually an hour and a half before the start, check for wind shifts or bends on your way to the start line. If it is a beat you can note shifts on the way. If it is a reach or run steer a straight-line compass course and check which way the wind has been changing relative to your sails. If you think there may be a difference in wind direction at the start line and the first mark you must go and check. If, for example, the wind is on 220 degrees at the start area and 240 degrees at the weather mark, it would

certainly pay to put in a long port tack after the start to take advantage of a veered wind bend.

If you cannot detect any wind bends then, on arriving at the start area, begin taking wind readings by either sailing close-hauled on both tacks and dividing your readings by 2, or by simply pointing your boat directly head-to-wind. Have a piece of white plastic stuck on your boat to write on with a chinagraph pencil and keep a record of the wind direction at five minute intervals to get a pattern of the wind oscillations, as in the following example.

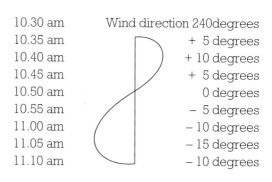

10.30 am	Wind direction 240degrees
10.35 am	+ 5 degrees
10.40 am	+ 10 degrees
10.45 am	+ 5 degrees
10.50 am	0 degrees
10.55 am	– 5 degrees
11.00 am	– 10 degrees
11.05 am	– 15 degrees
11.10 am	– 10 degrees

Having checked these oscillations a pattern will emerge and you will get an idea of what the wind is doing - if it is shifting around a mean direction or if it is gradually backing or veering. If it is the former it will pay to tack on the shifts, bearing in mind any tidal effects. If it is the latter and it is gradually veering (shifting clockwise), it would pay to play the shifts but stay over on the starboard side of the course to take advantage of the slowly veering wind. Always keep in mind the weather forecast and, most important, the way the majority of the fleet are going. In any decisions of strategy you must never leave the fleet, even if you are convinced your wind predictions are correct.

13 STARTING AND FINISHING

With half an hour to the start continue taking wind bearings and familiarise yourself with the conditions of the day by doing practice beats with other boats. Make sure you have the correct settings for the conditions and do not start making major alterations to your rig unless you have tried them before. Concentrate instead on sailing the boat as quickly as possible with what you know to be about right. Keep checking the wind and don't stray too far from the start line in case the wind drops. If the windward and gybe marks have been laid check that they are in the position the race committee says they

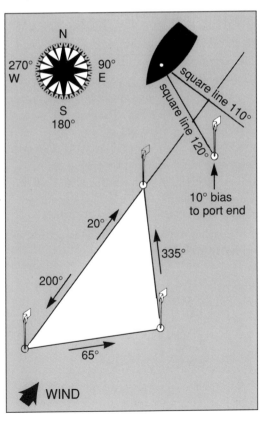

are by their magnetic bearings. Work out your compass bearings for the first reach, second reach and run, for example: Always remember that if you sail longer on starboard tack going up the beat you will sail longer on port down the run, and vice versa. Check also the wind direction in relation to your heading on both tacks (for example: wind direction 200 degrees; starboard tack 155 degrees; port tack 245 degrees). If you then start heading 135 degrees on starboard you will know the wind has backed to 180 degrees leaving the first reach very close and the second reach very broad. It will also mean a long run on the starboard gybe (probably all the way) and anybody who hasn't worked this out may gybe onto port if he can't see the mark and automatically lose places.

As soon as you have finally set your boat up for the conditions and decided what the wind is doing, go back to the start line and sail directly along it checking its compass bearing. Do this by starting off right by the committee boat and pointing straight towards the leeward end buoy. By knowing this bearing and the wind direction you can work out precisely the favoured end of the line.

In the diagram the wind direction is 200 degrees and the line bearing is 120 degrees. This line would be square if its bearing were 110 degrees, so it has a 10 degree bias to the port end.

Any good race officer would normally set the line with a 5 degree port-end bias so if he gives you a windward mark bearing of 200 degrees you would expect the line to

Pre-start manoeuvring. In light winds you can stay in position on starboard for two minutes before the start. To luff, pull the mainsheet in and ease the jib (top left); to bear away ease the main and back the jib (above).

You can also reverse – pushing the boom out to port sends you backwards and also makes the boat bear away (left). Pushing the boom to starboard makes you luff as you reverse. Once you're moving backwards the tiller acts in reverse, i.e. push it to bear away. So if you're approaching on starboard and get in irons, don't panic. Push the tiller away and hold it there until the boat reverses and falls onto starboard tack. Pushing out the boom will speed this up.

bear 115 degrees. Again know the wind direction because if it changes so will the start-line bias.

After checking the line try to get a transit between the buoy, the committee boat and a mark on land. If you can sight land then sail along the line away from it. Position yourself at the end of the start line and align the buoy and the committee boat with something such as a house or tree on the land. If you can do this you can then tell if you are over or below the line simply by glancing at your marker ashore. If you do

get a good transit, check that the line isn't moved between your sighting and the five-minute gun.

At the ten-minute gun

Once the ten-minute gun has been fired all your pre-start work (other than checking the wind) must end. You must also have eaten your food, taken plenty of fluid, filled or emptied your weight jacket, and worked out all the bearings to each mark.

Do not now cruise up and down the line risking being hit; instead go to the end of the line which is favoured and check the wind to make sure it is falling into its predicted pattern. Try to sight your transit to make sure neither end has drifted, and then make your way to your chosen position on the line.

If the line is biased then you must start as close to the favoured end as possible. Make your mind up before the five-minute gun which end it is and decide that you are the one who is going to get the best start.

At the five-minute gun

You are now in the most critical five minutes of the race and there must be no mistakes. Check the wind for the last time and make sure your wind readings are all adding up to some sort of pattern. This is most important in an oscillating wind as it dictates your first tack. If at five minutes to go the wind has veered by 10 degrees it will probably mean a 5 degree favour to the starboard end; this, however, won't be enough because after about ten minutes the wind may back 10 degrees giving the port-end starters a 5 degree advantage; 5 degrees at the port end would mean port-end starters crossing the fleet.

The port or pin-end start

If you have decided to start at the port end, your objective is to line up as late as possible while being certain of a slot. If the fleet begins to stack at 2 minutes to go, you will have to join them. Try to keep back from the line so you can manoeuvre, and can accelerate prior to the start.

Approach the line as close to the wind as possible, (but note you are not allowed to luff someone above close hauled before the start if he has mast-line on you). Your crew must hold both jibsheets ready to sheet or back the jib to control the angle of the boat. Sheeting the mainsail and easing the jib turns the boat into the wind, and easing the main and sheeting or backing the jib makes the boat bear away.

You must stay head to wind as you need to create space to leeward so that you can sail free and fast after the gun has gone. You will need, ideally, one boat length between yourself and the boat to leeward to ensure a good start. Any less will invariably mean the boat to leeward will force you into a lee-bow position. Any more is fine providing another boat reaching along behind the line doesn't fill the gap with 30 seconds to go.

All the time keep checking your position on the line by checking your transit or, if this is not possible, by keeping your bow in line with the bows of boats around you. The crew does the timing while you watch the boat to windward and the boat to leeward and anticipate their moving forwards or back. All the time be aware of the risk of being picked out as the boat 'most' over the line. This often happens in big fleet starts where the whole fleet is over the line but the race officer lets the start go and picks out the boats that were over further than the pack. Don't, however, play too safe and drop back behind other boats as the gap in the line will close and you will start in the second or third rank.

Assuming you have created a gap of at least one boat length to leeward with 10 seconds to go, your boat must be slowly moving forward hard on the wind. With 5 seconds to go you must be moving fast enough to hit the line on the gun at full speed. Timing is all-important, and your position relative to boats around vital. If you go for speed too soon you will risk poking your bow ahead of boats around and being disqualified. If you go too late you will be squeezed out by boats to leeward and windward and, within 10 seconds, be yards behind the fleet - then only lucky windshifts can save you from arriving at the first mark in the mid-fifties. Therefore if you are close to or even over the line, keep abreast of the boats to leeward and windward. The very second they sheet in their sails you must follow but do it faster and better so you edge your bow out into clear air. As soon as the gun goes bear away slightly and try to sail over the boat to leeward. Once you are over and past her you have made an excellent start.

If, however, you don't manage to sail over the boat to leeward you must hold your distance from her. Providing the boat on your weather is not going past you it doesn't matter if the boat to leeward goes ahead as long as you can hold up and stay clear of her lee bow. Try to hold this position as long as possible while you begin to check your compass to decide if you are on the right tack for your wind-shift sequence. If you are on a lift then you must hold on; if not then tack as soon as you are clear.

The starboard-end start

Starting at the starboard end can be dangerous in that a bad start means you have to tack to clear your air. This immediately separates you from the rest of the fleet going off the line on starboard presumably on a lift (as the wind must have shifted between the race officer laying the line and the start, making it a starboard-biased line).

Therefore when starting at this end you must be able to keep clear air and stay on starboard, waiting for the wind to back. The actual starting procedure is the same as for the port end, except that it is normally safer to stay to leeward of any bunch of boats fighting for pole position by the committee·boat. If you do get boxed in by boats around, escape by sailing further down the line looking for a nice gap that someone skillful has created for you. You must, however, recognise very quickly the danger signs of a bad start and get out at least forty-five seconds before the starting gun is fired.

Five-minute rule in operation

If a sudden death rule is in operation, start one-third of the way along the line from the favoured end, keeping your sails hidden from the race officer. You will not be pushed over the line in this less congested area.

THE GATE START

Starting any race through a gate is, in itself, reasonably easy; the skill is deciding where to start. Other things (such as tide and wind) being equal, you should start early if you are faster than the pathfinder, or late if she is faster than you. It is, however, very seldom that such options are open because invariably there are other factors to take into consideration.

Position relative to the fleet

Gate starts normally only happen in fleets of 100 boats or more. To start very early or late on an effective line of a quarter-mile could leave you in bad shape should the wind shift after the start. It is, therefore, good policy to start near the middle if you are confident of your boatspeed.

Apart from exceptional circumstances such as beating into stronger or weaker tide it is always the best strategy to start near the middle, get off the line and stay on starboard until you are clear to tack on any shifts without ducking behind other boats. If you can do this you are automatically in the top third of the fleet due to other boats sailing in bad air and having to cross behind starboard tackers. From a gate start you can never tack for at least two minutes, so you must ensure a good start and wait to play the shifts until the fleet has spread. Therefore fleet and speed strategy, rather than wind strategy, are the key to the first beat. Once you are clear to tack, get into the wind pattern and try at all times to cover the majority of the fleet. This ploy, together with reasonable speed, should always get you around the first mark in the top ten.

Going through the gate

If you think it will pay to start late then go through the gate when two-thirds of the fleet have gone, and if you favour an early start, when one-third has gone. Try to go through with as few boats around you as possible and, as in line starts, you much create space to leeward on your start. To achieve this you must clip the stern of the gate launch going at full speed hard on the wind. Do not come down to the launch on a reach, as when you round up you will lose distance to leeward and find yourself too close to the boat below.

If you do make a poor start and fall into bad air, your only option is to tack and bear away behind the other boats, going either all the way to the end of the gate, or tacking back in a space between starboard tackers. Depending on the wind, you may be lucky and get away into a reasonable position as you are only losing one boat length to each starboard boat, and usually you should be able to cross in front of slower boats or ones who have made a bad start.

FINISHING

Approaching the finish line, always aim to cross at the end of the line which would not be favoured were it a start line. In other words, as you are approaching the line imagine it to be the start and go for the opposite end to which you would start. Having decided which end is favoured, go for that end at full speed, just shaving either buoy or finish vessel. Don't cross the line in the middle as there is always a favoured end and you may lose places. If the wind is oscillating, keep off the laylines and try to position yourself so you can tack for the line and be on a lift. If you are almost level with an opponent, then a final luff head to wind, seconds before your bow crosses the line, could put you ahead of him.

PART 3

MASTERCLASS

14 WHAT'S IMPORTANT

Sailing is a complex sport. There are so many variables that people get bogged down with lists of things to do and skills that need improving. However, we reckon there are five key areas that you've got to get right. They are:

1 Time management
2 Attitude
3 Boat preparation
4 Boatspeed
5 Feel

1 TIME MANAGEMENT

Unless you're sailing full time you will have many demands on your time. How you resolve the conflicting demands will largely determine how well you do. The secret is to give yourself time to prepare and organise your programme. This applies to everything from booking accommodation, sorting the boat, getting tide and weather information, being at the start in good time, etc.

You can halve the work by dividing it between yourself and your crew, with tasks allocated according to skill level.

Also, we recommend a time management course. The main elements of this are detailed below.

But first, let's look at some of the myths of time management.

The first is that you can *manage* time. You can't! The clock keeps ticking whatever you do. All you can manage is what goes into your waking hours.

Next, many people feel that there's never enough time. Of course there is – for the *important* things. Note that important means just that - not irrelevant, or urgent, and certainly not fire-fighting someone else's crises. Simply delegate what's not important, and stick to the things that are important to you - like sailing!

There is also a feeling that the more you do, the better things will get. Fight that. Doing more of the wrong things only makes things worse. You use up all your energy, and the right things get squeezed out. Stick to what's important!

To manage your time properly you simply need:

● a needs list
● a diary
● enough people to delegate to.

Now organise your week and your day.

1 Block off in your diary the key things you must do for the next week.

2 Never start a day without having thought what you're going to do.

3 Have as few things as possible: never more than six per day.

4 Never put anything on the "to do" list unless you really are going to do it. This must be your contract with yourself: never leave without doing what you set out to do.

It's simple! Just:

Decide what you're going to do.
Do it.
Don't get diverted.

2 ATTITUDE

A complete course in sport psychology is obviously outside the scope of this book. The Fernhurst title Mental and Physical Fitness for Sailing may help, particularly with setting realistic goals.

It must be said that self confidence is a key to success. During a campaign you're going to have to follow your own route and try to get ahead of the opposition your own way - no-one else can sail the boat for you. That's not to say you can't listen to others - just make up your own mind what's garbage and what's useful.

Similarly, don't let anyone else psyche you out, or psyche yourself out. The best solution is self-confidence - just ignore their tactics.

3 BOAT PREPARATION

Your boat must be as good as the opposition's, if not better. Look particularly at the hull, foils and slot gasket.

One of the most tedious ways to lose a

race is through gear failure. Bolt through any fittings that take a high load - pintles, fairleads, vang, mainsheet, etc. Strength is more important than saving weight here. Before a race check all fittings thoroughly and if in doubt replace anything dodgy. When you're sailing home after a race make a job list in chinagraph pencil on the boat. Then fix everything when you come ashore, before you get into the bar.

4 BOATSPEED

Your sails *must* be in good order. Spinnakers tend to wear out first, followed by jibs. As a rough guide, for a serious campaign you'll get through 6 spinnakers, 6 jibs and 3 mainsails over a period of two years.

Calibrate the boat and log your fast measurements. Learn to 'change gear'

quicky, using these numbers, for an increase or decrease in windspeed.

5 FEEL

Calibration and fast numbers are all very well, but there are so many variables in waves, wind and tide that you need to be subtle and adapt to changes. The fast boys will do what they feel is right at the time, not stick rigidly to pre-determined settings.

Feel, seat of the pants, call it what you will is developed from experience. Reading, two-boat tuning, sailing blindfold and racing itself are all helpful in building feel. Whenever you have a chance, fiddle and see what happens: don't wait until you're going slowly to experiment. And remember, even if an alteration makes you go slower, you've still learned something. You won't make that mistake again!

15 TROUBLESHOOTING

If you find you're going badly try to analyse what's going on. How are we pointing? How fast are we going?

Can't point

1 Check rig tension - make sure it is sufficient.

2 Are the leech tensions of jib and main high enough? Do all the jib telltales lift at the same time?   If the top telltale breaks first move the fairleads forwards. Is the top telltale on the mainsail leech breaking 30 per cent of the time? If not adjust the mainsheet.

3 Check the mast bend control: the mast may be bending too much, losing lower leech return.

No speed to windward, but can point

1 The sails are probably too flat and the leeches too tight. So raise (or move aft) the jib fairleads. Straighten the mast and ease the vang.

2 Sail the boat upright.

No speed and can't point either

1 You need to check everything.

2 Get a professional to cast an eye over the boat.

3 Give up!

No speed on the reach

1 Spinnaker pole too far forward.

2 Centreboard too far down.

3 Too much vang. You need more twist.

4 Outhaul too tight.

5 Oversheeting main and/or jib.

6 Ease the cunningham right off.

16 CONCLUSION

There are basically three components that establish the speed of a boat: (1) the helmsman and crew, (2) the sails and rig and (3) the hull shape. In order of importance the helmsman and crew are easily first, followed by sails and rig and then hull.

It is imperative, if you are to be in the top 10 per cent at a championship, that your boat is right. Always remember that yards matter and anything that can gain or lose ten yards is important. Therefore be sure that your hull is fair; it is pointless spending hours sanding rudder and centreboard if your slot rubbers are old and worn and your self-bailers do not fit flush with the hull.

Only have fittings that you understand fully and know how to use. For instance, some years ago it became the fashion to use shroud levers. Only about one sailor in ten really understood their purpose, and much thought was wasted during the race on the mysteries of shroud levers. Never slavishly follow fashion; make up your own mind whether or not a piece of equipment will help you to get better speed and if you will, in fact, use it. In most championship boat parks there is enough `go fast' gear that doesn't add a yard to the speed of their owners' boats to fill a good sized chandlery.

Make certain that all your gear is in first-class working order. A surprising number of boats have cleats that slip, sheaves that won't turn, etc. Try a small squirt of WD40 on all your sheaves to make them run freely, and check and check again so that you can be sure nothing will break during the race.

Get your boat down to weight if possible, but don't get neurotic about it - 5 lb underweight or overweight never won or lost a championship. We have known people go to enormous lengths to bring a boat that is 5 lb over down to a minimum weight, then arrive at the starting area two minutes before the ten-minute gun totally unprepared mentally and with a thick head from last night's beer.

Rigs today have become fairly sophisticated and the number of controls is sometimes bewildering. If you aspire to the top ten of a big fleet you must understand the use and inter-relationship of various control and rig settings. For instance, spreader length and angle, vang, mast ram and mainsheet all affect mast bend. Mast bend affects sail shape, the slot, jib setting and so on.

It is beyond the scope of this book to explain the black art of boat tuning, but learn as much as you can from people who know - not from people who think they know or say they know, but from people whose results make you *believe* they know. Everyone from beginner to world champion is always learning something different about rigs so no one can tell you everything, but learn as much as you can. Tuning a boat to win, like most things that bring success, is a painstaking process, and that elusive extra speed is unlikely to be gained by simply buying a new suit of sails for the championships, sticking them up for the first time for the practice race and hoping they will make you go faster. Reading the Fernhurst books *Tuning your*

Dinghy, Tuning Yachts and Small Keelboats
and *Sailpower* will also help!

Old sails seldom win races, but tune your
boat to the new sails before you get to the
championship, and don't buy an extreme
suit that will be a winner in one set of
conditions - get a suit that can be set up for
all conditions by rig controls. Listen to your
sailmaker, and beware of pet theories -
your own or anyone else's; we have never
seen a championship won with a suit of sails
that was a 'design breakthrough'.
Improvement in sail design is, again, a slow
and painstaking process, so treat with
suspicion the 'magic formula' man.

The important thing to remember is that
the best hull and the best rig in the fleet will
not win if the helmsman and crew are
second rate, and the best helmsman and
crew will not win if they are not properly
prepared.

The only point in sailing is to get
enjoyment and satisfaction - not always the
same thing. Before you go to the
championships decide if you are going for
a 'jolly' and hope to do as well as you can
without too much hassle, or if you really
want to be as far up the fleet as possible. At
least 50 per cent of a big fleet know, before
the start of the first race, they have as much
chance of finishing in the top ten as of
winning the pools. These lads go for a
good sail, good company, a good laugh and
usually, plenty of ale. They are the
backbone of any class and, without them,
there would be no championship - always
remember this.

On the other hand, if you want to win you
must be in top physical and mental shape
for five or six hours a day for six days. So
live quietly at the championships, go to bed
early, get up early and prepare everything
quietly and methodically so that you are not
panicked into last-minute hitches.

Don't be discouraged by big reputations

and by the people who seem to you
unbeatable. If you, your crew and your
boat are all properly prepared and your
pre-race routine is correct, if you keep
clear of protests and you are a good club
helmsman, you are almost sure of a place in
the top 20 per cent. Don't let one bad
result, a disastrous start or a slow boat
passing you put you off. There is a lot of
sailing in a week's championship and
positions ebb and flow like the tide. It is
amazing how fortunes fluctuate during six
or seven races.

At almost every championship one of the
fancied competitors spoils his chances by a
stupid mistake. Make sure you *know* the
course (sometimes race officers do the
unexpected). Don't forget tallies and five-
minute rules. Take all the gear out you will
need: some years ago an Olympic
helmsman sailed a championship race
without a spinnaker pole - he had
inadvertently left it ashore!

Respect your fellow competitors -
especially the lads down the fleet - don't get
drawn into private feuds, and avoid trouble
like the plague - it destroys your
composure and balance and ruins your
concentration. If you are involved in an
incident, put up your protest flag and then
forget it until you are ashore - don't get
involved in acrimony during the race.

Finally - sail hard, sail to win, keep a
sense of proportion at all times ... and enjoy
yourself.

Good luck!

Also published by Fernhurst Books

The Catamaran Book *by Brian Phipps*

Catamaran Racing *by Kim Furniss and Sarah Powell*

Championship Laser Racing *by Glenn Bourke*

Crewing to Win *by Andy Hemmings*

First Aid Afloat *by Dr Robert Haworth*

The International Fourteen *by T.J. Vaughan*

Knots and Splices *by Jeff Toghill*

The Laser Book *by Tim Davison*

Laser Racing *by Ed Baird*

Mental & Physical Fitness for Sailing *by Alan Beggs & John Derbyshire*

Mirror Racing *by Guy Wilkins*

Racing: A Beginner's Manual *by John Caig & Tim Davison*

Racing Crew *by Malcolm McKeag*

Racing Skipper *by Robin Aisher*

The Rules in Practice 1993-96 *by Bryan Willis*

Sailing: A Beginner's Manual *by John Driscoll*

Sailing for Kids *by Gary & Steve Kibble*

Sailing the Mirror *by Roy Partridge*

Sailpower *by Lawrie Smith and Andrew Preece*

Sails *by John Heyes*

Tactics *by Rodney Pattisson*

Tides and Currents *by David Arnold*

Topper Sailing *by John Caig*

Tuning Yachts and Small Keelboats *by Lawrie Smith*

Tuning Your Dinghy *by Lawrie Smith*

Weather at Sea *by David Houghton*

Wind Strategy *by David Houghton*

Fernhurst Books are available from all good bookshops and chandleries. In case of difficulty, or if you would like a copy of our full catalogue, please send your name and address to:

Fernhurst Books, Duke's Path, High Street, Arundel, West Sussex BN18 9AJ